T0148955

IN THE
NATIONAL INTEREST

General Sir John Monash once exhorted a graduating class to 'equip yourself for life, not solely for your own benefit but for the benefit of the whole community'. At the university established in his name, we repeat this statement to our own graduating classes, to acknowledge how important it is that common or public good flows from education.

Universities spread and build on the knowledge they acquire through scholarship in many ways, well beyond the transmission of this learning through education. It is a necessary part of a university's role to debate its findings, not only with other researchers and scholars, but also with the broader community in which it resides.

Publishing for the benefit of society is an important part of a university's commitment to free intellectual inquiry. A university provides civil space for such inquiry by its scholars, as well as for investigations by public intellectuals and expert practitioners.

This series, In the National Interest, embodies Monash University's mission to extend knowledge and encourage informed debate about matters of great significance to Australia's future.

Professor Margaret Gardner AC
President and Vice-Chancellor,
Monash University

DAVID ANDERSON

NOW MORE THAN EVER: AUSTRALIA'S ABC

MONASH
UNIVERSITY
PUBLISHING

Now More than Ever: Australia's ABC
© Copyright 2022 David Anderson
All rights reserved. Apart from any uses permitted by Australia's *Copyright Act 1968*, no part of this book may be reproduced by any process without prior written permission from the copyright owners. Inquiries should be directed to the publisher.

Monash University Publishing
Matheson Library Annexe
40 Exhibition Walk
Monash University
Clayton, Victoria 3800, Australia
https://publishing.monash.edu

Monash University Publishing brings to the world publications which advance the best traditions of humane and enlightened thought.

Proceeds from the sale of this book will be used to support the work of various charities.

ISBN: 9781922633118 (paperback)
ISBN: 9781922633132 (ebook)

Series: In the National Interest
Editor: Louise Adler
Project manager & copyeditor: Paul Smitz
Designer: Peter Long
Typesetter: Cannon Typesetting
Proofreader: Gillian Armitage
Printed in Australia by Ligare Book Printers

A catalogue record for this book is available from the National Library of Australia.

The paper this book is printed on is in accordance with the standards of the Forest Stewardship Council®. The FSC® promotes environmentally responsible, socially beneficial and economically viable management of the world's forests.

NOW MORE THAN EVER: AUSTRALIA'S ABC

I am never far from someone who reminds me how much they care about the ABC. A few months back an old friend rang and asked me how I thought the ABC was travelling. She sounded worried about the ABC's long-term future, a concern I see shared by other ABC supporters. It is true that in real terms, ABC funding is 30 per cent lower than it was in the mid-1980s. This year, the ABC's operational funding is more than 10 per cent lower in real terms compared to 2013–14. Meanwhile, our regular critics in the Australian media continue their campaign to try to discredit the ABC as an institution. Internationally, there have been well-organised calls to 'defund' public broadcasters altogether, including in Canada and the United Kingdom, and this right-wing agenda is being amplified by social media. The globalisation of news and entertainment is creating major new challenges for all media organisations, along with many opportunities. As I assured my friend, these are not issues that are being taken lightly. How could they be?

But it is equally important not to lose sight of the bigger picture. The ABC is Australia's leading digital news source. The number-one national radio network. The number-one daytime channel for Australian children. The ABC is Australia's most trusted source of news and analysis, easily the most trusted media organisation in our country, and one of our most trusted public institutions overall. It is the undisputed home of Australian stories and thoughtful science, arts, religion and education programming.

The evidence for the ABC's strength and success in Australian life is overwhelming. The vast majority of Australians put their trust in the ABC, rely on it, value its importance to democracy, and think of it as a reliable source of news, information and entertainment. It should be a matter of national pride that, over nine decades, a multigenerational community of talented artists, reporters, broadcasters and storytellers has shaped this unique and irreplaceable Australian institution.

This book captures my thoughts on the place and future of the ABC in our national life. It is inevitably, in part, a personal perspective. I have spent my working life within the ABC's corridors, surrounded and inspired by passionate and dedicated colleagues. I want to give a sense of the ABC in action, the scope and scale of our contribution to the civic lives of our cities, towns and regions, and to the private lives of countless individuals right across this country. The ABC also generates jobs and stimulates economic activity throughout this country. It is a driving force in the national media and production ecosystem. In dozens of big and small ways, the ABC makes Australia a better place in which we can live together as citizens, experience and evolve our shared culture, and build a brighter democratic future for our children and grandchildren.

Certainly, the challenges faced by the ABC are very real, but they don't substantially raise the stakes for those of us who are fortunate enough to be part of the current generation of ABC leaders. We already know we must aim high to play our role as a champion of Australia's identity and community. In an era of low trust in institutions and media, the ABC must promote social inclusion and cohesion, and advance our democratic values. As global giants offer more entertainment choices, and commercial investment in Australian content declines, the ABC needs to, and will, play an even bigger role in sharing and promoting Australian stories and culture.

It's a big agenda, one that no other organisation in our country can fulfil. So we will continue to advocate for a budgetary envelope that gives us the financial stability and confidence to comprehensively undertake these tasks on behalf of Australia. We know that if we continue to win and maintain the support of the Australian people, we can never lack confidence in the future.

I hope that in reading this book, all those who care about the ABC in Australian life will be reassured that we are ready for the challenges we are facing today and which we will face tomorrow, and for anything else the twenty-first century throws at us. We know it matters. The ABC is more important to Australia's wellbeing than ever before.

AUSTRALIAN IDENTITY

I grew up with the ABC in Adelaide through the 1970s and 1980s. ABC Radio was always on at our place, and Philip Satchell on 5AN was the soundtrack to our mornings. Satchell, who sadly passed away just last year, was always at ease, whether questioning cranky federal ministers or conversing with classical musicians. He was a master of the unnerving pause, which meant that his interviewees almost invariably said just that little bit more than they intended. It was an enormously positive idea of Australia that Satchell brought into our family home: an Australia in which big ideas were valued and debated, and local issues were of paramount importance.

The ABC began in 1932 as an Australia-wide network of independently operated radio stations, pulled together as a conglomerate. ABC Radio is still the spine of the ABC today. Each weekday we broadcast fifty-two live breakfast shows around the country. In a world of strident opinions and hardline positions, the voice of the ABC is open-minded, curious and empathetic. It hosts the conversations that seek to clarify and find common ground, rather than polarise and divide. ABC broadcasters remind Australians that they are not isolated but connected to something bigger, from the incidents of daily life in their local area, to their shared hobbies and interests, to the unfolding of our national story at home and on the world stage. No wonder these broadcasters often hold a special place in their communities—somewhere between local personality, community organiser and chief cheerleader.

ABC staff like Andrew Schmidt, our chief of staff in Broken Hill, in the far west of New South Wales, are proud to represent their communities every day. A while back I was wrapping up a visit to Broken Hill, just about to head out to the airport, when I shocked Andrew by admitting that I had never been to the Palace Hotel, the iconic location where scenes from *The Adventures of Priscilla, Queen of the Desert* were filmed. It didn't matter that we were running late; Schmidty insisted we have a tribute beer in the famous front bar. He wasn't going to let me leave town without a quintessential Broken Hill experience, one that I would be sure to remember and recommend to others. As indeed I do.

There have been so many other legendary local ABC broadcasters. Sadly, we recently lost Russell Woolf in Perth, a broadcaster who embodied the spirit of the ABC. But that spirit is carried forward by broadcasters like Belinda King in Launceston, Ewan Gilbert in Orange and Nadia Mitsopoulos in Perth. And Ian McNamara, of course. Macca is a friend to Australians at home and across the world.

Then there is ABC Radio National, where the big countrywide conversations about politics, policy, life, the arts, religion and education become intimate personal experiences for listeners, via great broadcasters like Margaret Throsby, Geraldine Doogue, Phillip Adams, Daniel Browning and Andrew Ford. When Fran Kelly announced last year that she was leaving her RN Breakfast post after seventeen years, there was an outpouring of affectionate protest and heartfelt appreciation.

This feeling of trust extends beyond personal affiliations with ABC broadcasters to trust in the ABC as a local and national institution. Every Christmas, for example, the ABC's Hobart and Launceston offices work with local charities to host the Christmas Giving Tree Appeal. Local families and communities bring a gift or a donation to put under the tree in the foyer of those offices, because they know that the ABC will do the right thing for those most in need. This is a tradition repeated across the country.

Community partnership with the ABC also happens at a wholly informal level. A few years ago I was in the ABC office in Perth during one of the increasingly severe bushfire seasons. I became curious about a large pile of boxes stacked up in the foyer. People were spontaneously leaving canned foods, blankets and non-perishable items with the ABC, on the correct assumption that we would distribute them quickly and wisely. The community's generosity was so great that the local Perth team had to hire a small forklift to clear the area every day or so. Now we have brought our charity work under one banner: ABC Gives. Last year we raised more than $800 000 through fundraising drives across ABC Radio.

The importance of the ABC to regional and rural Australian communities has only increased over recent years, especially as so many towns have seen a decline in traditional institutions and services. The local ABC offices matter more than ever when local government offices, banks, churches and newspapers have either disappeared, shrunk, or digitised their services, severing that physical connection with place and loosening the bonds of community trust. Since 2019, nearly

200 media outlets and newsrooms have closed, contracted or merged across our nation, creating a worrying rise in 'news deserts'.[1] This shift mostly has been driven by the loss of advertising revenue for traditional media and the urban consolidation of the major players.

But our ABC teams are still there, getting out and reporting the local stories that matter to Australians living beyond the capital cities, and putting their stories on the national stage. Our reporters tell me of locals who, spotting the ABC logo on the side of their car, flag them down to have a chat about a few things on their mind. In Launceston a while back, I noticed the office had installed a street-level window so that questions from the public could be easily answered. As I walked by, young ABC staffer Fred was answering questions from a gentleman who saw the ABC as such a useful source of knowledge, he wanted to know how to contest his parking fine.

My first job at the ABC was in the Adelaide mailroom. Soon after that I was working across various administrative areas, trying to help out wherever and however I could. That's how I met Margot Philipson, then head of the ABC's children's department, which at that time was located in Adelaide. Margot was one of the many iconic ABC executives I've met over the years whose passion and pride in what they do inspires everyone in their orbit.

The first thing you learn at ABC Children is that it takes children's content incredibly seriously. All the content produced by the ABC for kids is informed by a deep, expert understanding of their wellbeing and positive development as future citizens of Australia. Children and adolescents use television and other media experiences to gain a better understanding of themselves, to safely rehearse situations they may one day experience, and to develop interpretative and behavioural skills for their relationships with others. Research also affirms the value for children of seeing characters who look and sound like them—they benefit from stories that are genuinely representative of their own experiences in the world.

Over the years, ABC Children has created a legacy of memorable experiences for Australian kids, from *Bananas in Pyjamas* to the skivvy-wearing *Wiggles*, who recently celebrated thirty years of success, and their long-running relationship with the ABC, by releasing a greatest hits album, *We're All Fruit Salad!* Another more recent and well-loved addition to our stable is *Little Lunch*, filmed in Melbourne, about six primary-school children navigating the highs, lows and dilemmas of the school playground. *The Inbestigators*, about some school-aged crime-solving sleuths, is often played on TV through ABC iview by my nine-year-old before school (due to our household policy of 'no device' during the week).

Then there is *Play School*, which is in a league of its own. *Play School* first went to air in 1966 and is now the longest-running children's show in Australia, and the second-longest-running in the world behind the BBC's *Blue Peter*. Its longevity is a tribute to the ABC's preschool experts who write scripts that seamlessly marry play and development, and to the many talented Australian entertainers who've presented the show over the years. The *Play School* live-concert format is very popular and deceptively simple: two *Play School* presenters and a pianist, plus favourite toys like Big Ted, Humpty and Kiya. These affordable, uncomplicated concerts take place in local civic centres, school halls and RSL clubs all over suburban, regional and rural Australia. They have enchanted hundreds of thousands of Australian children while reinforcing their sense of identity, belonging and community.

And now we have *Bluey*, arising from this same commitment to excellence in children's entertainment. *Bluey* has quickly become a global phenomenon, winning acclaim and numerous international awards. When trying to sum up just how big a milestone *Bluey* has become for children's viewing around the world, one colleague put it to me this way: 'There's *Thomas the Tank Engine*. There's *Peppa Pig*. But now there's *Bluey*. *That* is how big it is.'

Bluey, for the uninitiated, is a blue-heeler pup growing up in her close-knit family of four.

The show is so Australian that one of its episodes is called 'Dunny'. Disney+ has chosen to honour this authenticity by keeping the original Australian voices for broadcast to overseas audiences. Which is why young North American children have increasingly been heard to say 'G'day', much to the surprise of their parents. *Bluey* models modern parenting at its finest, with two engaged parents, a lot of laughs and a fair amount of just getting through the day. It also, at its best, achieves the grace of a work of art. One episode, 'Sleepytime', was named by *New York Times* reviewer Margaret Lyons as one of the best TV episodes of 2020. In any genre. She wrote:

> Plenty of little-kid bedtimes require delicate choreography. In just seven minutes, this 'Bluey' segment captures the gorgeous vastness of child-hood imagination, a dreamy outer-space ballet … the frustrations of 'Can I have a drink of water?' in the middle of the night and the ineffable grief within the mortality of parenthood … What a great show.[2]

In May 2021, during a hiatus between COVID-19 lockdowns, and after about 100 shows in its hometown of Brisbane, the first live show of *Bluey* came to Sydney. There was a traffic jam of prams outside the Opera House foyer that day as suburban parents and international film stars rubbed shoulders, and the mood was buoyant. The physical gathering brought a new dimension to the *Bluey* experience and an opportunity for a joyous communal reaffirmation of Australian identity. As live entertainment kicks back into gear after the long pandemic lockdowns, I predict that tickets to live-action *Bluey* will be some of the hottest in town.

Increasingly, however, we cannot take it for granted that great Australian stories will automatically be available to us. On the contrary, in a globalised world, dominated by international streaming services led by cashed-up giants like Google, Amazon and Netflix, there is a very real risk that Australian stories may be crowded out—even here at home. Domestic free-to-air TV networks are no longer required by regulation to air any Australian children's programs. None at all. This means that the ABC today stands almost alone in its commitment to original, excellent Australian children's content and broadcasting.

There have been some government financial incentives for international streamers to invest in local production, which provides an opportunity to showcase Australia's formidable production capabilities. But even a high-quality, very success-ful production like *Clickbait*, a miniseries that was filmed in Melbourne, was not about Australia at all, but set in Oakland, California and helmed by US actors. That does little to promote our sense of Australian national identity at home or elsewhere in the world.

The ABC will never accept the prospect of Australia's culture being weakened, diluted, or packaged into some bland semi-globalised tem-plate. We will always tell the authentic Australian stories designed by, for and about us, and situated across our magnificent and unique continent. There's much more we could do, and we won't ever need a specific quota as incentive to do it (as some have suggested). In fact, setting a minimum level of output for ABC television production (or any production for that matter) would reduce our flexibility to appropriately and independently allocate funds across all ABC activities, including news and regional services. It could set a precedent for further interventions in the allocation of the ABC's budget. The amount of Australian content that the ABC commissions is purely a function of our budget, not a matter of intent.

And here's something else we know. It's the very Australianness of our stories that makes them resound so powerfully beyond our shores. The more specific, local and unique the story, the more broadly it is likely to resonate. When audiences worldwide are immersed in the colourful Melbourne of *Jack Irish* on Acorn in the United Kingdom, or beguiled by the humour of *Please Like Me* on Netflix, or captivated by the Queensland adventures of *Bluey* on Disney+, they are getting to know our landscapes and cultures via quality stories commissioned and nurtured by your national broadcaster.

We each discover and shape our identities as we make the individual journey from childhood to adulthood. But a process of evolution also occurs at the national level as we adapt our collective identity over time. The voice of the ABC in 1932 sounded terribly British. We took our tone and style straight from the BBC. Despite this, the first chairman of what was then the Australian Broadcasting Commission (now Corporation), Charles Lloyd Jones, still felt obliged to warn Australian audiences not to expect the 'high broadcast standards of London' given that Australia was a colonial culture that could not possibly compete with the BBC.

The shifts away from this were at first gradual, then accelerated by the big cultural and political upheavals of the late 1960s and 1970s. The ABC's daily state-based current affairs program *This Day Tonight* commenced in 1967. It was based on a British program but took on a newly confident Australian tone with its inquisitive style, Australian accent, and sense of humour and experiment. Another milestone I think of is the

ABC's *Norman Gunston*, played by the remarkable Garry McDonald. Gunston was the world's worst talk-show personality, flummoxing Australian and international celebrities alike, and representing a new national confidence through an ability to laugh at ourselves and our pretensions.

Today, we have a dramatically bigger Australia. Our population has doubled since 1970, within the lifetime of many Australian adults. Between 2005 and 2020, the population expanded by around five million to more than 25 million people. This huge shift, much of it over a comparatively recent period, has resulted in rapidly expanding suburbs and outer-urban areas across our major cities. Families are dealing with the gritty problems of daily life in middle Australia: servicing the mortgage, paying the utility bills, educating the kids. As the population continues to grow, the ABC must be on the spot to tell the stories that matter. That's why we are aiming to have 75 per cent of our content-makers located outside our Ultimo, Sydney headquarters by 2025. It's all about connecting with, and listening to, our emerging, changing communities and making sure we cover the issues that are relevant to people's daily lives. It's also about telling Australians what's going on around their country, and fostering coast-to-coast conversations that help develop a shared sense of the nation's interests and goals.

We are increasing our presence in places like Sydney's Parramatta and Brisbane's Ipswich, where we already have bureaux. We have established 'pop-up' bureaux in Brisbane's Sunnybank, Sydney's Liverpool, Victoria's Box Hill and Geelong, Swan in Perth, and New Norfolk, Moonah and Sorrell in Tasmania. We have more pop-ups scheduled for Werribee, Campbelltown and the outer suburbs of Adelaide. These pop-ups are a collaboration between our local radio and ABC News teams, focused on outer suburbs in metropolitan cities that are under-represented in media coverage.

The impact of climate change, combined with Australia's rapid population growth and broader geographic dispersal, means we are inevitably going to see more human impacts from more frequent and severe natural disasters.

The ABC was right there for Australian communities during the catastrophic bushfire season of 2019–20. One in two people in the affected areas said they used the ABC as their main source of information throughout the protracted ordeal— often via their car radios when the power went out—while 60 per cent of people in the bushfire regions reported that information from the ABC helped keep them safe.[3] As the then deputy prime minister Michael McCormack simply said, the ABC saved lives.[4]

It's a grim reality that access to some form of emergency broadcasting for most of the year is now likely to be the new normal, and the ABC will need to bolster its capability to provide such essential services. Whether it's teams in our state newsrooms, or local radio in capital cities or across forty-eight regional locations, people will turn to us for what may be life-saving information, and we will be ready to provide it.

A profound duty and priority for Australia and for the ABC is continuing the unfinished work of reconciliation between the traditional owners and custodians of this ancient continent and non-Indigenous Australians. The ABC has a legacy over many years of helping Aboriginal and Torres Strait Islander people to share their stories with the nation. We are now intensifying our efforts to strengthen Indigenous storytelling across all our platforms. We aim to provide more employment and business opportunities for Indigenous Australians. And we are doing our part to normalise the use of Aboriginal and Torres Strait Islander names in our news reporting and social media briefs, and through initiatives that teach and explore Aboriginal languages and names.

In 2012, I was lucky enough to be involved in the ABC's decision to commission the movie-length drama *Mabo*, on the remarkable life of Torres Strait Islander Eddie Mabo. Eddie Mabo left school at the age of fifteen but went on to become the lead figure in the historic High Court challenge that overthrew the fiction of terra nullius and changed our nation. It is a great film and was nominated for a Logie. On the way to the awards ceremony, I found myself sitting in a car with Eddie's seventy-year-old widow Bonita, their daughter Gail, the movie's director Rachel Perkins, and actors Jimi Bani and Deborah Mailman, who played Eddie and Bonita (that night, Deborah would be awarded the Logie for Most Outstanding Actress). Bonita said a few words to Gail in language, and Gail said, 'Mum wants a song.' The group sang a birthday song in language for Bonita, and it was a privilege to be there for that special moment. I have no doubt that the more we hear the languages, stories and songs of Indigenous Australia, the stronger and richer our culture will be.

The ABC Charter tasks us with contributing to a sense of national identity and reflecting the diversity of our nation. Diversity can take many forms, of course, including gender, age, language, disabilities, sexual orientation, religious beliefs and more. The ABC fulfils this duty with storytelling that deploys wit, innovation, compassion and, most of all, optimism.

Take *Employable Me*, based on a BBC format. It features job-seekers who demonstrate that having a physical disability or neurological condition does not make them unemployable, but rather makes them *highly* employable for certain roles. The idea was presented to us when I was in a position to champion it. Some people said, 'You know what David, this is not going to rate very well.' But it was an important job for the ABC to be doing and we were absolutely going ahead. Like many Australians, I know people who are living with autism spectrum disorder. So I took particular notice when, as *Employable Me* went to air, I was contacted by an advocacy network that specialises in placing people with ASD into jobs. There had been a massive spike in requests for the employees they represented: the numbers went from something like five people per month to over a hundred in the first month of the program. That's the kind of positive social impact the ABC can have.

We know there is plenty more that can, should and must be done on diversity and inclusion. And we are always inspired and motivated by the benefits generated when we get it right. As it turned out, *Employable Me* did rate very well, and

the impact across the community was invaluable—
so much so that we commissioned a second series,
along with series two of *Love on the Spectrum*,
which is another ABC success story. Who else but
the ABC would bring to the fore these extraordinary Australians who are now loved, admired and
understood by so many?

A standout for the ABC over recent years has
been *You Can't Ask That*. This is a program with
a uniquely Australian, no-frills way of dealing
with the myths and fears that can build up around
those who are perceived to be different, those who
find themselves misunderstood or pushed to the
margins. When casting for its seventh season in
2021, *YCAT* invited Australians who identified as
heroin users, bogans, adult entertainers, dementia
sufferers and those with post-natal depression
to take a seat on our program. Participants are
courageous, being asked to answer anonymous,
sometimes crudely honest questions sent in
by our viewers. It sounds high-risk, and in the
wrong hands, it could be. But with the ABC
creating a space in which individuals can speak

for themselves, own their own stories and air them safely, the process is often profoundly cathartic.

You might be surprised to learn that this daring program is already the most successful ABC format in our history, adopted and localised in countries around the world, from Israel to Canada, from Belgium to the United States, and with more to come. Already, thirty seasons of *YCAT* have been delivered across ten international productions in nine different languages, including Arabic, and seven more territories have taken options on the format. These international broadcasters are telling us that this is a much-needed show in their countries for greater mutual understanding, and that content like *YCAT* makes the world a better place. Some markets are also looking at developing a version of the program specifically for kids. *YCAT* has become a uniquely Australian gift to the world.

At home, what matters to the people of Australia will always be what matters to us. *Australia Talks* is a survey developed by the ABC in collaboration with social and data scientists at the University of

Melbourne, plus an advisory panel of academics from other Australian universities. The survey is designed to help the ABC understand more about our audiences, so we can respond even more effectively to their interests. In *Australia Talks 2021*, 60 000 people from across every state and territory and every federal electorate generously answered questions about their attitudes, behaviours and experiences.

There were many fascinating insights, but one sentiment stood out for me: 80 per cent of our respondents said they thought Australia was the best country in the world. ABC audiences are glad to be Australian. It *matters* to be Australian. And they are endlessly curious about, and inspired by, each other. Richard Fidler and Sarah Kanowski's *Conversations* are in-depth, hour-long interviews, usually with an Australian who has an interesting story to tell. It is our most popular ABC podcast: last year there were five million or more downloads on average each month. Our long-running *Australian Story* is an award-winning and much-loved documentary series with no narrator and no agenda, just the stories of Australian lives told entirely in people's own words. I watch with wonder as Executive Producer Caitlin Shea and her team deliver this outstanding program each week. A more recent entry is *Back Roads*, hosted by Heather Ewart, who celebrates the unique passions and characteristics of outback communities. Heather brings us the stories of people who are proud to be Australian wherever they may be.

No nation stands still, of course. They inexorably move forward through time, shaping and being shaped by new realities. Since World War II, Australia has taken waves of refugee populations, people fleeing persecution, from Europe to Vietnam. Refugees in recent years have included arrivals from war zones in Africa and the Middle East. Australia today is still an immigrant nation, with all the change and dynamism that implies. As at 30 June 2020, 30 per cent of Australia's population had been born overseas. And it is a core task for the ABC to recognise, fully reflect and celebrate this diversity while honestly exploring its effects and implications. Today, there is also a significant Australian diaspora living overseas, estimated in pre-COVID circumstances at around one million people.[5]

Mobility within Australia is increasing, and that changes the nation too. Over the years we've seen a big boost to the populations of our major cities due to immigration. Now, in a counter-trend that looks to have been accelerated by COVID-19, significant numbers are moving out of the capital cities to regional cities and smaller towns. According to the Australian Bureau of Statistics, in the March quarter of 2021, the net loss from the capital cities to internal migration was the largest on record.[6] The ABC's *Movin' to the Country* is following this trend, taking an intimate look at how these life-changing decisions play out for individuals and their new communities.

Australia's age profile has greatly changed as well, partly because life expectancy has so dramatically increased. In the seventy years between 1950 and 2020, life expectancy for women rose 18 per cent to eighty-four years.[7] Life expectancy over the same period for men went up even more notably, by 22 per cent, from age sixty-seven to eighty-one.

In 2020, *Old People's Home for 4 Year Olds* showed the unexpectedly joyous impacts of play dates between some older Australians in aged care and a bunch of inquisitive preschoolers. The program was developed with a team of experts in geriatric health and wellbeing, child development and physiotherapy. It was not only a ratings success in Australia but went on to win an International Emmy Award. Just as importantly, it unlocked a productive national discussion about the isolation and loss of confidence experienced by older Australians, and how we as a community can come together to address it. A second season broadcast in 2021, made with the same care and expert attention, focused on opportunities to increase the emotional wellbeing of senior Australians who are living independently.

In any nation that is so quickly evolving, the issues and choices that confront citizens must also change. Australians will continue to face new economic questions, new geostrategic dynamics, new technologies and risks, new social priorities, and the overwhelming challenge of climate change. The ABC's role is not to take a policy position on the best way forward but rather to host the debates that must inevitably take place along these new frontiers. We are not afraid of facilitating the difficult conversations: indeed, we are ideally placed to do so. We recognise that people will bring their diverse perspectives to discussions about the future shape of our nation. By opening up those conversations, by letting more people air their views and be heard by other Australians, we contribute to a stronger environment for forging broad agreement on the way ahead.

Of course, there are those who would prefer it if the ABC didn't play such an active part in engaging with the Australian community on potentially contentious issues. Some think we should leave it to the political class to initiate the important conversations about our identity and our future. But the reality is that Australians have regularly proved to be more open to the prospect of considering social change than the politicians who represent us. On issues such as the public apology to the stolen generations, marriage equality, and the ethics of voluntary euthanasia, the legislators have largely followed Australian opinion rather than led the way. That's not a criticism, by the way, simply a fact. But it only reinforces the importance of the role played by the public broadcaster.

We also know that if the ABC is to be truly effective in representing the diversity of experience in Australian life, we must ourselves achieve greater diversity. With a broader pool of storytellers, we will be better equipped to reflect the breadth and depth of the changing Australian experience. ABC women are leading the way, making up 54 per cent of our employees today. You can see and hear the positive effect of having more equal numbers of women in senior journalism and editorial roles. Important stories that until recently might have been glossed over or simply ignored, but which matter to all Australians—and are vitally important to Australian women—are now being told: stories about the mistreatment of our elderly in aged care, sexual misconduct and misogyny in

Parliament House, the division of labour in the home, and the grave economic disadvantage faced by older women.

In terms of seniority, women are well represented at the two top levels of the ABC below my role as managing director, but there is still more work to be done to achieve equality for women in the mid-levels of our organisation. And we have more to do on diversity and inclusion more broadly, both because it is the right thing to do and because it will make us more effective and relevant as a public broadcaster.

The ABC nurtures social cohesion and national unity through the sensitive ways in which we recognise and explore Australia's differences. We provide the safe forums—from talkback radio, to *You Can't Ask That*, to *Q+A*—that open up the discussion, and we help Australians consider the implications of the realities we face and the choices that lie ahead of us.

In so doing we help all Australians accommodate their past and present to a broadly shared vision of the future. Through all our programs, we make an important contribution to evolving and protecting the rich, capacious, distinct Australian identity embracing us all.

AUSTRALIAN DEMOCRACY

Once every three years, Australians go to the polls for a federal election. The day starts with volunteers setting up at dawn on the east coast and ends with the polls closing at dusk in the west. It's always a Saturday, on a date carefully chosen by the governing incumbents for its typically good weather nationwide and to avoid a vote-losing clash with the near-sacred troika of footy, cricket and the races. Across our continent, it's fundraising time, with cake stalls, raffles and sausage sizzles at local schools, church halls and childcare centres. It's a day for enthusiastic party members to press how-to-vote pamphlets into the hands of hesitant voters, while candidates wander around the polling booths looking for hands to shake. And it's a day for Australian citizens who patiently queue for their turn to vote as they idly gossip with their neighbours and grumble at the cumbersome length of the Senate ballot. We live in a country that has the good fortune and good management to be able to take this low-key democratic ceremony for granted.

The federal election is always a very big deal at the ABC. Months of planning go into it. Our rolling news coverage across television, radio and digital from our locations around Australia is both a celebration of our democracy and an assurance of its integrity on its signature day. We offer uninterrupted coverage, unrivalled experts, spotlights on marginal seats, and live crosses to candidates. For many years we hosted live debates between the leaders of the two main political parties, although more recently our invitations to successive prime ministers to participate in this democratic ceremony have been declined. Ideas have been put forward for a federal election 'Debates Commission' to govern election debates. As the national broadcaster, the ABC stands ready and eager to take part in developing a workable model.

The national tally room is a thing of the past but, as counting begins, the ABC's Antony Green is on hand to offer his essential data and sharply worded insights. A panel of current and former political figures join the ABC's political team to analyse the results. When the count is done, the loser makes a few rueful concession remarks and the victor gives their first speech as the incoming or returning prime minister. This peaceful transition of power culminates in the first parliamentary sitting, where all the elected members take their seats in Australia's Parliament House.

Australia's federal election represents the high point of our national democratic cycle. But a strong democracy doesn't just automatically happen once every few years. It relies upon ongoing respect for, and assent to, the democratic way of Australian life. And today this faces new challenges. Here, as across the world, we have seen the rise of a largely unregulated, often unmoderated social media marketplace, coincide with a precipitate decline in trust, not only in traditional media but in other conventional sources of authority, such as governments, banks and churches. This is having a significant damaging impact on opinion formation. It enables and fosters extremist views, distrust in officialdom, conspiracy theories and anti-science beliefs. And this can, and increasingly does, have worrying real-world consequences.

We all saw the frightening scenes in the US Capitol on 6 January 2021, when newly elected American representatives were forced to run and hide from a violent mob. That mob didn't magically coalesce on a single day. For years, disaffected groups of Americans saw their grievances magnified into anti-democratic beliefs, encouraged by elements of old and new media. The horde's deluded sense of legitimacy on that dreadful January day was fuelled by the exhortations of the outgoing president himself.

At the ABC, with ninety years almost behind us, we have a strong sense of history. We know things can go wrong gradually at first, then turn bad very quickly. Australia must never take its own peaceful electoral transitions for granted. We need to take care of democracy every single day: by recognising the primacy of individuals and their rights and obligations as citizens, upholding equality of opportunity for all in the community and before the law, and being tolerant of differences and opposing ideas. Sustaining this democratic system requires constant vigilance—that means consistently accountable government, appropriate checks and balances to prevent the abuse of power, and, most of all, the engagement of informed citizens.[8]

A significant body of global research confirms the vital role played by independent public broadcasting in fortifying democracy. People in countries with public service broadcasting are better informed about their government and politics, have more positive civic attitudes and greater trust in others, and are more likely to engage in democratic politics and action. What's more, it's thought that the benefits of public broadcasting have a 'rainmaker' effect, with higher levels of social trust, 'even among the individuals who do not habitually watch public service channels'.[9]

When the ABC's first Australian parliamentary broadcast took place back in 1946, Ben Chifley was still prime minister. Parliamentary broadcasting immediately made Australian politicians uncomfortably aware that they were operating in the public eye, and that sense of accountability still prevails today. When I go to Canberra, members of parliament will tell me, not always with unrestrained gratitude, that constituents tend to contact them after listening to or watching what goes on in the parliament via the ABC. I remind them that's got to be a good thing: active and engaged citizens strengthen the bonds of our democracy.

The ABC has also had a long-running commitment to Canberra's National Press Club addresses, where politicians and leading Australians from all spheres of national life are given the time and space to lay out their thinking on complex questions, and to respond to journalists who are themselves made more conscious of their responsible role because they identify themselves to the audience. Through those Wednesday lunchtime broadcasts, we make a pro-democratic experience available to any Australian with access to a TV set or a laptop, whoever or wherever they may be. We offer Australians the chance to participate in the democratic process far more often than that single trip to the local school or church hall every few years on polling day.

A powerful unifying element in any democracy is a sense of shared values and historical memory. Australians turn to the ABC to mark the key dates in the national story. We always cover Remembrance Day. On Australia Day we cover both the smoking and flag-raising ceremonies. We enthusiastically celebrate the Australian of the Year ceremony. ANZAC Day in April is especially important, and the ABC marks the associated services both in Australia and, whenever possible, at the key locations overseas. Coverage of most of these ceremonies would simply not be viable for the commercial broadcasters. But they matter enormously to many Australians, they contribute to our sense of shared destiny, and they reflect the ABC's overall unifying mission in our democracy.

Former ABC chairman Jim Spigelman, also a former chief justice of New South Wales, made an observation in his 2017 farewell speech that has stayed with me. He said, 'The ABC has to treat its audience as citizens, not consumers; as people with rights and duties, not just wants and needs.'

Citizenship starts early with the ABC. We are the only broadcaster trusted by education experts around Australia to sit side-by-side with them in the delivery of our children's education. In 2020 the ABC Education Department went into over-drive to help Australian kids keep learning through lockdown. The ABC immediately expanded its educational resources on TV to ensure those children without access to computers were not left behind. As agreed with the departments of education in Victoria and New South Wales, the ABC took cameras into classrooms and filmed teachers giving mini-lessons on literacy, numeracy and other subjects. Annabel Astbury, Head of ABC Education, says it was remarkable how immediately capable all the teachers were in front of the camera. The content they created is still in demand today.

Our COVID-19 crisis support has com-plemented our ongoing work with state education departments and school teachers to create a wide range of content suitable for learning at school or at home. Our ABC Education online portal has regularly hosted more than 5000 educational videos and teaching resources, plus educational games, for use by schools and students. Our free resources cover Australian and world history, science, current affairs and much more. They've been refined by feedback and experience to be of maximum practical use to teachers in the classroom. We are now in the process of further developing the portal, and this is not just a one-way effort: we encourage kids to speak to us and each other about their own identities and experiences, with competitions and other opportunities to express themselves as thoughtful emerging citizens. It's a learning community.

The ABC's *Behind the News* program has been going since 1968 and it is now the world's longest-running children's news program for the informed and engaged Australian citizens of the future. Indeed, it's the second-longest-running current affairs program behind *Four Corners*.

BTN breaks down current issues and events in a kid-friendly way, while also providing the background information that isn't always offered by other news bulletins. We make *BTN* widely available on the companion website, but also via ABC iview, TikTok, Facebook and Instagram, to give access to the maximum number of people.

In a vibrant democracy, acts of citizenship take many forms. The ABC is an enthusiastic promoter of citizen science, one of the most enjoyable and productive types of democratic participation. Take our *Hoot Detective* project, a partnership between ABC Science, the Australian Acoustic Observatory, Queensland University of Technology and the University of New England. The Australian Acoustic Observatory, the world's only bioacoustics observatory, has placed 400 recording devices in 360 sites across Australia. Its recordings are building an important archive of vocal animal activity, helping scientists to understand which species are located where in Australia, and how our fragile environment is changing in response to invasive species and climate change. For National

Science Week 2021, the *Hoot Detective* project called on all 'citizen scientists' to help them identify the locations of five species of native Australian owls: those notoriously private nocturnal birds that are mostly readily identified by their distinctive calls.

The project works like this. Our citizen scientists are first taught to recognise the calls of the five owls by listening to them online. They then listen to ten-second grabs from a large catalogue of night recordings and note online which owl calls they believe they hear, if any, plus the sounds of other native creatures. These small individual contributions will save scientists many years of work in cataloguing their audio archives and will be used to improve the algorithms which detect species calls. When I last looked, more than 5000 sessions by citizen scientists had been logged online, and more than 21 000 owl calls had been identified. Our partnership with Australian universities in the *Hoot Detective* project, as in so many others, reflects the confidence and trust the scientific community invests in the ABC.

Reliable and accessible information is central to any successful democracy and society. The ABC's commitment is to provide information that is defined by its accuracy, balance and completeness; and coverage that is both timely and able to stand the test of time. Indeed, I often remind our people that it's more important to be accurate with the news than to be the first to publish. It's a point reinforced by scientist and Australian Nobel laureate Professor Peter Doherty, who has explained why we must defend quality publicly funded broadcast media like the ABC: 'In Australia, where everybody is required to vote, it is essential that reliable, honest information should be available to all.'[10]

The unfolding of the COVID-19 pandemic reinforced this imperative. The ABC quickly positioned itself as a media leader in giving Australians the clear, unadorned, factual information that they could rely upon in a confusing and stressful time. *Coronacast*, led by Dr Norman Swan and Tegan Taylor, became a top-rating podcast. The infographics of Casey Briggs on ABC News provided clear statistical information to help people form their own assessments of the ongoing crisis and its management. The ABC assembled a multi-disciplinary team of science journalists, true crime producers and audio specialists to produce *RN Presents … Patient Zero*, a podcast which won the Australian Museum Eureka Prize for Science Journalism, and which helped audiences understand major disease outbreaks—where they begin, why they happen, and how the world found itself in the middle of this particular one.

It is this consistent delivery of reliable and timely information that explains why the ABC consistently ranks as Australia's most trusted media outlet. This has been confirmed by numerous independent surveys, our own tracking, and the 2021 *Digital News Report* produced by the University of Canberra's News and Media Research Centre. Furthermore, the ABC is one of the top ten most trusted brands across any Australian industry. It's the only media organisation on that list, the only government organisation on that list. This is a rare achievement.

The ABC not only devotes itself to accurate and impartial reporting, it also helps to bolster truth standards more broadly across our society. Since 2017, the ABC has maintained a jointly funded partnership with RMIT University to produce a *Fact Check* service that determines the accuracy of claims by politicians, other public figures, advocacy groups and institutions engaged in the public debate. This arrangement combines academic excellence and the best of Australian journalism to inform the public, and to ensure the facts are verified through an independent, non-partisan voice.

This status in national life means that Australians will entrust their stories to the ABC, confident that they will be treated with sensitivity and discretion. In 2018, for example, *Four Corners* ran a two-part special investigation into the treatment of the elderly in aged-care homes. This was led by the highly respected ABC journalist Anne Connolly, who devoted years to this hitherto underreported issue. Connolly and her team turned to Australians for the real story,

crowdsourcing their research insights. More than
4000 people shared their experiences of aged care
with the ABC because they trusted that we would
do the right thing. Many of those who came forward were professionals in the industry who were
deeply concerned by what they had seen. Family
members also spoke out with disturbing accounts
of neglected residents. Here was citizen journalism
in action, and it not only informed that ground-
breaking *Four Corners* report but also led to an
historic royal commission.

It's not only older generations of Australians
who trust the ABC. Due to the well-established
relationship between triple j and young
Australians, the triple j *Hack* team was well
placed to collaborate with *Four Corners* on an
investigation into the rise and implications of
new dating apps. Young people told triple j about
their experiences in their own frank words. Some
of the stories were shocking—the investigation
progressively revealed how predators were using
dating apps to lure young victims. This program
also led to lasting policy change, including greater

security, and reporting features on apps like Bumble and Tinder.

A vital element of maintaining community trust is the ABC's dedication to journalistic objectivity. This is non-negotiable. Our reporters are expected to put aside their personal views to report on issues fairly and impartially. We do not accept the proposition, promoted by some, that 'fair and impartial' reporting means allocating the same degree of weight to positions on the 'left' or 'right' of the political spectrum on any issue, regardless of any gross imbalance in expertise or credibility. On the long-term consequences of climate change, for example, the ABC will give more weight to the informed view of leading scientists working in the field than to those with no scientific knowledge but vested economic interests in fossil fuel extraction.[11] We clearly distinguish between opinion and fact, and we believe that, to again quote Professor Doherty, 'You're welcome to your own opinions, but not to your own facts.' We follow the weight of the evidence. Our job is to search for the truth and deliver it, knowing the truth has no political alignment. And we are equally unafraid to amend or correct our position as new information comes in.

With this approach, without fear or favour, the ABC has an unrivalled track record in Australia of investigative journalism in the public interest. Numerous royal commissions can be attributed in whole or part to *Four Corners* over its sixty-year history. Since 2016 alone, ABC *Four Corners* investigations have contributed to the formation of five royal commissions: *The Protection and Detention of Children in the Northern Territory* (2016–17); *Misconduct in the Banking, Superannuation and Financial Services Industry* (2017–19); *Aged Care Quality and Safety* (2018–21), as mentioned above; *National Natural Disaster Arrangements* (2020); and the *Murray-Darling Basin (South Australia)* (2018–19). Royal commissions are not called lightly—these are major exercises, costly, time consuming and authoritative. They are only called when compelling information comes to light that requires the highest judicial examination, when it really matters.

You'll note the diverse range of subject matter that is covered here, from environmental issues to corporate malfeasance and administrative failure. There is no underlying agenda with our reportage. It's about identifying the story, following the evidence, and holding those in power to account for their actions.

Modern democratic societies protect and nurture their national civic values and way of life internally. But they also form external coalitions with other democracies to find solutions to shared regional and global problems, and to collectively defend their values. Australia plays a major role as a responsible democratic partner in the Asia-Pacific, and for more than eighty years ABC International has been an important vehicle for our diplomacy in the region. Through broadcast television and radio, websites and apps, ABC International tells Australian stories, reports fairly and fearlessly, teaches different generations to speak English, and delivers critical information in times of crisis, including throughout the COVID-19 pandemic. In our Asia-Pacific Newsroom in Melbourne, a

dynamic network of local and international jour-
nalists writes and reports on events across the
region, with news broadcasts in both English and
Tok Pisin, a broadly used Melanesian language;
ABC news websites are also provided in Bahasa
Indonesia and Mandarin.

ABC International often joins with suitable
partners to promote development in our region. In
2021 we worked with the International Foundation
for Electoral Systems to combat misunderstanding
and disinformation concerning COVID-19 across
the Pacific. After appropriate training, senior
journalists and communicators led workshops in
seven countries across the region. These sessions
provided local journalists and social media
influencers with new skills and tools with which
to verify information, and to help them report
accurately on COVID-19.

One of the strongest contributions you can
make to democracy is to model good democratic
practices at work. At the end of 2019, the ABC
partnered with the Fiji Broadcasting Corporation
and the University of the South Pacific to produce

a Pacific edition of our public affairs program
Q+A. It was chaired by the ABC's Tony Jones,
and the panel included the director of the Pacific
Fisheries Agency; Fiji's attorney-general; a former
prime minister of Tuvalu; Australia's then minister for international development and the Pacific,
Alex Hawke; and a prominent Pacific women's
rights activist.

In Australia, of course, our key political figures
regularly appear in the media to face questions from
journalists. They also make themselves available
to programs such as *Q+A* to respond to audience
questions. However, this routine of normal democratic life was a new experience for Fiji. Audience
members raised topics directly with political
leaders that were sensitive and significant: the risks
of Chinese economic influence, the increase in
illegal fishing, continuing violence against women
and girls, the deadly measles epidemic, and the
problem of anti-vaccination prejudice.

The program displayed civil society at its
best, where elected officials agree to be directly
challenged by difficult questions from the

public, and are expected to respond on the spot. The conversation was robust but peaceful and courteous, and feedback on the program was overwhelmingly positive.

Essential to the ABC's democratic credibility is its genuine independence. Just as the High Court and the Reserve Bank maintain authority and public trust because of their strictly defined independence from political interference, so does the ABC. In fact, Australia's reputation for strong democratic institutions stems largely from this tradition of the careful separation of powers. It is in no-one's interest to see any erosion of the ABC's independence, which has various dimensions. The public funding that supports the ABC means there is no actual or perceived pressure to tiptoe around issues that may affect sponsors or advertisers. Lacking subscribers, the ABC can't be subtly tempted to focus on any particular audience segment or demographic with content that caters to one perspective on the world.

The ABC is opposed to any proposal for a so-called 'external' government-appointed ABC ombudsman exercising powers beyond the current role of the Australian Communications and Media Authority. Other major public broadcasters like the BBC and CBC have no comparable external role and it would raise the possibility of government interference, significantly degrading the ABC's independence and its capacity to perform its democratic function.

We can't take democracy for granted. We can't take public broadcasters for granted either. Unfortunately, public broadcasters and independent journalism around the world are increasingly under pressure. The ABC has joined with seven such broadcasters—the BBC and the national broadcasters of France, Germany, Canada, New Zealand, South Korea and Sweden—to form a global task force to defend the values of public media, in order to safeguard the future of healthy democracies.

Independence means just that, independence, but it certainly does not mean a lack of accountability. The ABC is always accountable to the people of Australia. This accountability is expressed every day through the roles of the six directors (plus the chair) appointed by the government to the ABC board for five-year terms, as those positions become available. The managing director and one staff-elected representative also have seats on the board. The ABC's governance structures are robust and ensure its operating integrity, as it plays its part in our democracy.

AUSTRALIAN CREATIVITY

When I first started working at the ABC in Adelaide in 1989, a new world opened up for me. Wherever I looked, I saw a rich creativity that was expressive of our Australian culture and values. I straight away put my hand up to try out wherever I could. I discovered that, even if I wasn't going to make it as a creative myself, I could contribute to the ABC in another way. Because great and emerging creative people need their champions. They need defenders who will provide a safe space for their risk-taking and establish the practical frameworks within which they can advance their projects. They need backers who understand that even failure can be a waystation on the road to creative success.

Today, there is far broader recognition of the role of creativity in all of human evolution and progress. Certainly, the greatest minds of the twentieth century were clear about the value of creativity, ranking the achievements and some of the methods of the arts alongside the natural and social sciences. Albert Einstein thought it was important 'for the life of the nation to be fertilized and enriched by the achievements of art and science'.[12] Having campaigned for its creation, Einstein's admirer, the economist John Maynard Keynes, became the first chair of the Arts Council of Great Britain; it would later become the model for the Australia Council for the Arts. Introducing the council to the British people on BBC Radio in 1945, Keynes explained why the ways of artists were so important to the broader fortunes of the culture:

The work of the artist in all its aspects is, of its nature, individual and free, undisciplined, unregimented, uncontrolled … The artist walks where the breath of the spirit blows him. He cannot be told his direction; he does not know it himself. But he leads the rest of us into fresh pastures …[13]

Creativity—the bold advance into fresh pastures, new territory—is today a matter of consuming interest to scholars of all kinds, who seek to unlock the breakthrough mindset shared by the great artists, scientists, inventors and entrepreneurs. We've probably seen more scientific and technical change in the past 100 years than in the previous 1000, and the pace is only accelerating as we look ahead.[14] Think tanks, businesses and governments alike acknowledge creativity, as well as adaptability and innovation, as a vital source of comparative advantage as they look to succeed in a fast-changing world.[15]

At the ABC, creativity defines us. We innovate in our programs, in our formats, and in how we adapt and use technologies to inform, educate and entertain. We were ahead of the game with

ABC iview, which was Australia's original and leading on-demand service. Some questioned our decision to offer a 24-hour news service, but that too was ahead of its time: it is now an essential part of what Australians look to us for. We are continuing to engage thoughtfully with new platforms so that we reflect the media-consumption patterns and preferences of all our audiences, and particularly reach out to young people. Most of all, we nurture all the creators: the writers, actors, designers, musicians and producers who dream up new worlds for our imaginations, who challenge us, celebrate our differences and enrich our lives.

Take the ABC's extraordinary role in Australian musical life. The ABC started out in 1932 with music flowing through the then commission's veins. There were the various symphony orchestras on air and on tour, but the ABC also catered to diverse and popular musical tastes, with a military band and two full-time dance bands plus professional choirs. Jim Davidson's ABC Dance Band, with its catchy swing music, was the most popular band in Australia before World War II.

The ABC in those early days was clearly the dominant force in the Australian musical ecosystem, but we are arguably just as culturally influential in music today, not least because so many others have vacated the field. I sometimes imagine our whole nation would fall into an empty silence—or just be crowded out by the music of other places—without the ABC's passion for Australian sounds. The ABC plays more Australian music than any other broadcaster by a wide margin, nurturing new talent across all genres and promoting it on our various radio and digital channels: ABC Jazz, Double J, ABC Country, triple j and Unearthed—plus ABC Music, which is Australia's largest independent record label. We have supported the careers of countless artists through the highs, lows and inevitable lulls of the creative life. We have been essential to the rise and success of country music in Australia and overseas; for instance, we are a stalwart partner of the Tamworth Country Music Festival and have had a thirty-year partnership with country artist Lee Kernaghan. Last year we once again teamed up with the Country

Music Association of Australia to produce a four-CD set celebrating Australian country greats across the decades: there was Lee Kernaghan, of course, plus Slim Dusty, Redgum, Beccy Cole, The McClymonts, Kasey Chambers and many more.

Then there's ABC Classic, which continues to bring together a passionate community of classical music lovers. If you think classical music is just for wealthy older Australians, you're wrong. The audience profile for ABC Classic has actually become *younger* in recent years, with hundreds of thousands of under-fifties listening and interacting with the channel. Here, too, there is always an Australian flavour. In 2020, *Classic Choir* brought together more than 1500 Australians to give the premiere performance of multitalented Yorta Yorta composer and soprano Deborah Cheetham's new carol *Christmas with You*. Broadcasts across ABC Radio, RN, News Breakfast TV and ABC Classic reached millions in the run-up to Christmas. The story of Australian music is a credit to our wealth of musical talent, but it also relies upon the ABC's institutional backing of creativity to help them flourish. There's one case study above all that tells that story.

Let me take you back—way back—to 1975, when Double J first took to the airwaves in a cramped underground studio in Sydney's Darlinghurst. Announcer Holger Brockmann cleared his throat, admitted to his nerves, and then played the first song: 'You Just Like Me 'Cos I'm Good in Bed' from Skyhooks's album *Living in the 70's*, a song that had been banned on commercial radio. That was an outrage right there. He followed up with the Rolling Stones's 'Sympathy for the Devil', confirming the station's scandalous alliance with the tastes and music of a new Australian generation. From Skyhooks to Paul Kelly, The Saints to The Go-Betweens, Midnight Oil to Mental as Anything, Double J proudly championed Australian music. As one member of that team, Gayle Austin, recalled: 'We wanted to establish a truly Australian identity. We chose to speak in our own accents and honour our own culture.'[16]

In 1980, Double J moved from AM to FM and became triple j, celebrating with a massive free concert in Sydney's Parramatta, and inaugurating the ABC's ongoing commitment to live, sweaty Australian rock music for anyone who wanted to be part of it. Since 2004, triple j has almost annually taken the country's biggest musicians to put on a massive, free event in Australian regional and outback towns like Cowra, Mount Isa, Geraldton, Mildura, Tumby Bay, Alice Springs, Sale, Collie, Port Pirie and Natimuk. A proud nation of headbangers.

Creativity begets more creativity. *Like a Version* began in 2004 as a weekly segment on triple j's 'Mel in the Morning' program. Artists were invited into the studio to play two songs: one of their own and the second a cover version. Artists responded with enthusiasm to this left-of-field creative assignment. All performances were filmed by triple j and made available on its website and YouTube channel. This experiment has grown so much in popularity over the years that ABC Music has now released several compilation albums of *Like a Version* performances ... and a number of big international artists have joined in too.

The success and longevity of triple j has always been about its intense bond with its young Australian audience. As one of the team insists, 'Others can get old, but we stay young with our audience.' The Hot 100 started in 1989 and now, more than thirty years later, the Hottest 100 is a massive annual event, when what triple j immodestly describes as 'the world's largest musical democracy' votes for its song of the year. Consider this: nearly three million Australians over the age of sixteen listened to the 2020 Hottest 100 live on triple j. And nearly seven million Australians over sixteen said they engaged with the Hottest 100 in some way. Music matters to us as a nation. Our musical preferences. Our music.

In 1995 there was still more musical path-finding with the arrival of Unearthed. This was a live competition to uncover exciting musicians from regional and rural Australia. Over the next ten years, artists like Grinspoon, Missy Higgins and Killing Heidi were 'unearthed' and set on the path to big careers. By 2006, new technology was making it possible for musicians to create relatively high-quality songs in their own homes. And so, in the next innovation, the triple j Unearthed website was launched. Young musicians can simply register and upload their songs. It is a simple yet revolutionary way for artists to get their music out to the world and to be found by new admirers. This pipeline is particularly valuable to artists from diverse backgrounds, or those with original artistic approaches, who might otherwise find it hard to get noticed. Unearthed also runs numerous professional-development competitions, making it possible for young artists to get practical support with everything from music video production to gigs at major music festivals.

And still the innovations continue. Unearthed High was launched in 2008, an opportunity for all those kids with big dreams who were playing bass and trying to look cool in their local high school bands, but also a recognition that many of the most musically talented start very young. In 2018, The Kid Laroi, a supremely gifted young Indigenous boy from a housing commission flat in Sydney's Redfern/Waterloo area, put up three songs on

Unearthed High along with a profile of himself that simply said, '14 with a dream.' Today, still under twenty years of age, The Kid Laroi is acclaimed as a global music sensation, one of the rare occasions when that description is no exaggeration at all.

Of course, the value of Unearthed in all its forms is about more than finding the stars of the future. It provides a place where all young artists can feel recognised and validated, where creative expression and enjoyment matters for its own sake, and where Australians connect with each other and with communities of music lovers and fans. A happy side effect for the ABC is that it is also bringing in the next generation of our audiences.

The fact is that no media organisation does more than the ABC to promote all the arts in Australia. Our ongoing commitment includes RN's suite of programs, like *The Stage Show*, *The Art Show*, *The Book Show*, *The Music Show*, *The Screen Show*, *The Bookshelf*, *Lost and Found*, *Blueprint*, *Stop Everything!*, and Indigenous program *Awaye!* Last year the ABC launched a new weekly arts program, *Artsfest*, on ABC TV Plus, alongside feature-length documentaries and live performances of music, ballet, theatre, film and opera. In all that we do, we tell the ongoing story of Australia. Successful nations don't lose interest in themselves. They tell and retell their own stories, and through that process they mature and evolve over time. An Australia without the ABC would be like a person who has lost interest in their own inner life.

When it comes to screen production, the ABC remains the nation's largest commissioner of new Australian content. In the three years up to 2021, the ABC commissioned 170 TV productions in-house and more than 250 productions externally. Where external partners were involved, the ABC's financial contributions were matched, plus some, by our partners. That's a reflection of the ABC's strong reputation and capacity to bring in funding for worthwhile projects. Nearly 6000 people worked directly on these productions from within and outside the ABC, and a further 2300 jobs were supported across Australia.

The economic and wider benefits of ABC creativity are extensive. *Rosehaven* is an offbeat comedy about two friends who find themselves living in a fictional picturesque town in rural Tasmania. In the making of the five seasons of *Rosehaven*, millions of dollars were spent on Tasmanian wages, goods and services. The series showed off the tourism attractions of the region and raised the profile and credibility of Tasmania as a production centre. *Mystery Road* is a multi-award-winning and internationally successful series starring Aaron Pedersen, about an Indigenous police officer walking the difficult line between black and white cultures. The series is mostly set in the awe-inspiring landscapes of the remote north of Western Australia. Locals were cast as extras, the cast and crew spent time with local schools, many Indigenous local businesses were involved, and millions of dollars were spent on local goods and services.

One of the most powerful moments of my own career was when we did an outdoor screening of our drama series *Redfern Now* for the community in Redfern. I was part of a breakthrough production that all involved felt immensely proud to bring to the people of that community, and to the entire nation.

And here I must mention comedy, that most explosive and risky form of creative programming. Over the years, many, if not most, of the great Australian comedians and comedic teams have been nurtured or supported by the ABC, not surprisingly most of them at triple j, performers such as Roy and HG, Judith Lucy, Wil Anderson (no relation), Mikey Robbins, Merrick and Rosso, Scott Dooley, Sam Simmons and Tom Ballard, and of course The D-Generation, Working Dog and The Chaser.

One of the fascinating trends over recent years in Australia, but also in the United Kingdom and elsewhere, has been to watch these and other comedians, like Kitty Flannigan and Celia Pacquola, develop into accomplished actors, beloved broadcasters, and presenters of factual and entertainment programs.

A lot of sketch comedy has disappeared from free-to-air commercial Australian screens in recent years. It's not cheap to produce. It can easily fail, or tip over from edgy into offensive. Because sketch comedy tends to be closely bound to current events, it often has a short shelf life. This becomes a commissioning factor at a time when the hunt is on for content that can be recycled over time as part of an on-demand catalogue. The ABC would commit more resources to comedy if we had the funds, but in the meantime we are still taking the risks and nurturing Australian talent.

In my role as Managing Director, I spend a lot of my time figuring out how to protect and nurture the creative excellence of this country through the power of the ABC. Australians already know and love so many of the talented on-screen and on-air individuals who have worked with us. Less known is that behind the scenes there have been, and still are, many more creative stars, highly respected in their fields around the world.

Among them is Sally Riley, ABC Head Drama, Entertainment & Indigenous, who is accelerating Indigenous and diverse storytelling at the ABC with great shows like *Mystery Road*, *Stateless*, *Total Control* and, more recently, *The Newsreader* and *Fires*. Sally's achievements over the course of her illustrious career saw her inducted in 2020 into the Academy of Motion Picture Arts and Sciences, the most prestigious film body in the world, which means she gets to vote for the Oscars.

Natalie Waller, Head of ABC Music & Events, is also the Chair of the Board of ARIA (Australian Recording Industry Association), and she is one of the few non-American members on the board of the famed Country Music Association based in Nashville. In 2021, she was recognised in the United States for her outstanding work in supporting country music's marketing development beyond America.

Michael Carrington, Director of ABC Entertainment and Specialist, is an Australian who grew up in the outback NSW town of Parkes. He has spent much of his extraordinary career in the United Kingdom, particularly as a trailblazer in shaping children's programming—his numerous awards include a BAFTA (from the British Academy of Film and Television Arts) and an International Emmy. He nurtured *Bluey* through its long development phase into the global but very Australian hit that is has become. This is all potent cultural capital for our whole nation. It not only enriches the Australian cultural ecosystem but is admired and sought after around the world.

Creativity in modern life is increasingly multi-dimensional. The next big waves of scientific and technological innovation are likely to arise out of cross-disciplinary exchanges: bringing together smart ideas across widely different fields, from robotics and artificial intelligence to genetics, quantum computing and more. This surge in creative interconnectivity will amplify and accelerate the innovation agenda over the coming years.

In many ways, the ABC has long acted as a conduit for the exchange and interweaving of very different disciplines to the national benefit. In these pages I've already described some of our many collaborations with scientific, educational and academic institutions and communities, with wonderfully surprising outcomes like *Hoot Detective* and *Old People's Home for 4 Year Olds*. These are not shallow contacts but real engagements that productively connect creators and innovators with each other, and with the broader community. A snapshot of the collaborations the ABC has undertaken in any given year might also include the CSIRO, Department of Foreign Affairs and Trade, National Australia Day Council, national galleries in New South Wales and Victoria, Sydney and Canberra writers' festivals, WOMADelaide, Garma Festival in the Northern Territory and the Australian Red Cross.

The ABC's contribution to Australian creativity is often taken for granted, but that is to underestimate what has been achieved over many years. We act as a national creativity grid, a network transmitting and receiving culture and content, and delivering life-affirming boosts of creative energy and ideas around the Australian body politic. We know how to give protection and support for risk-taking, within the appropriate frameworks. We work with extraordinarily talented people to solve creative problems and find new possibilities along the way. There will occasionally be failures, but we will never just play it safe. The successes are many and resound for the nation. The present-day custodians of this much-loved and trusted institution are positioning the ABC as Australia's creative and cultural powerhouse for future generations.

THE WAY AHEAD

The ABC was created at a time of media scarcity in 1932. The need was to improve a widely dispersed nation's access to news, information, education and entertainment. During the ABC's first broadcast, from the General Post Office Building in Sydney's Martin Place, Australian political leaders emphasised the range and significance of the ABC's mission. Liberal prime minister Joseph Lyons declared that the ABC was there to 'provide information and entertainment, culture and gaiety, and to satisfy the diversified tastes of the public'. Labor Opposition leader James Scullin warned that broadcasting under national control should *not* be an instrument of oppression or misrepresentation. Earle Page, Country Party chief, said plainly that where broadcasting may be a luxury to city folk, to country people it was a necessity, especially for news on commodity prices.

Now, ninety years later, just as Lyons projected, the ABC not only provides information and entertainment for all Australians, it also celebrates our nation's diverse hobbies and interests, from citizen science to religion and ethics, balcony gardening to cricket, children's entertainment to factual podcasts, edgy comedy to engrossing drama, and great music from classical, jazz, children's and country, and, of course, the music of young Australia.

Today, as James Scullin enjoined, the ABC remains fiercely protective of its editorial independence, delivering Australia's most trusted public interest journalism through investigative reporting, fact-checking, public health and safety information, and emergency broadcasting.

And Earl Page would surely be pleased to know that nearly a century after that first broadcast, the ABC remains an essential resource for rural and regional Australians, with forty-eight of our fifty-six bureaux in regional locations around the country. And we still provide updates on commodity prices for hardworking Australian farmers and graziers.

While the ABC was created out of a need to address media scarcity, Australia has now moved into a world of multimedia abundance. We are living through a revolutionary set of changes in news, media and entertainment. On-demand viewing services like Netflix, Stan, Apple and Disney+ are in a global race for viewers. Their offerings will be bigger, more lavish productions, scaled up to compete with the finest cinematic productions. Apple spent approximately US$6 billion on content in 2019. Amazon spent US$11 billion in 2020. And Netflix was planning to spend US$17 billion in 2021. These are huge numbers. Meanwhile, specialist services like Foxtel's Kayo offer sport on demand; Spotify and Apple Music promise unlimited musical choice; and YouTube offers a lottery of user-generated material and, increasingly, curated content. Traditional TV and radio formats, with their fixed linear schedules, are figuring out how to best compete with these myriad choices and the instant gratification of paid and free sources available via phones, laptops and home theatre screens.

News has also changed forever. Not only can Australians readily access international news online, overseas news providers have targeted the Australian market with Australian content and are experimenting with ways to win and keep their Australian customers. As a result, local news providers have seen their traditional audiences decline and lost precious advertising revenue to platforms like Google and Facebook. One response, as in the Nine Entertainment and Fairfax case, is to consolidate and cut back, while in the regions of Australia, as I have mentioned, many smaller news outlets have simply disappeared.

And a further layer of invisible transformation is underway. Internet search engines and social media today operate as gatekeepers between news and entertainment organisations and their potential audiences. The big streaming companies aim to retain loyalty and increase spend through powerful algorithms that mine customer data to help them 'personalise' their offerings and retain loyalty. So far, in my experience, this tends to result in offers of more of the same. If you decide to rewatch a single favourite James Bond film on Apple, you can expect months of promotions for all the rest.

We can also see that, while the options available to Australians beyond the ABC for their news, information and entertainment have multiplied, more is not always better. We will need the ABC to play its part in addressing new types of information, media and social deficits: loneliness and disconnection, fake news and conspiracy theories, a distrust in the efficacy of our democratic processes.

I began this book by acknowledging that many Australians who care about the ABC are concerned about its future. I am not surprised by this, given the way in which our critics conveniently overlook, ignore and disregard the totality of the ABC's contribution right across the nation, every single day. But the critics don't deter us. We know that for democracy to flourish, a nation's citizens must have an independent source of truth they can turn to—one that is unwavering, unbiased, and committed to providing the accurate, relevant information they need. This is the core role played by the ABC. And any attempts to interfere with, or undermine, the independence of the ABC, by either political or commercial players, must and will be resisted at all costs.

It's my view that the best defence for the ABC against attacks on its legitimacy, or interference in its operations, will always be the ongoing support of the Australian people. I believe we can count on that support because now more than ever, the ABC matters to Australia.

It matters to all of us who have turned to the ABC during the COVID-19 pandemic as an essential source of facts and clear analysis, explaining the work of our scientists and government officials, and giving us the confidence to come together, do the right thing for ourselves and our communities, and stay the course.

The ABC matters to people in rural and regional communities, especially those who must now rely almost solely on the ABC for news and information. For them, the ABC is an essential service, especially during times of natural disaster and extreme weather events.

It matters to all Australians who care about integrity in our institutions. Our public-interest journalism leads to royal commissions, inquiries, and changes in legislation that fix wrongs and improve lives.

It matters to the kids who rely on *Bluey* and other ABC programs not just for entertainment but also to help develop their sense of self, family, friendship and community.

It matters to schoolchildren who are learning about the world around them, how their society works and how we are developing as a nation.

It matters because the ABC is a unique platform for enriching conversations, and for the expression of our inner lives through the arts. No other organisation can claim to have contributed to Australian culture in so many different ways as the ABC.

It matters because, in a world where extreme movements and dictatorships are on the march, the independent ABC sets a global standard for quality journalism and the democratic freedom of the press.

It matters because our democracy at all levels is made stronger by the work of our journalists who hold those in political power to account, who question legislative changes and policies, and who ensure that Australians are fully informed about political promises and the consequences when these are enacted.

The ABC matters to Indigenous Australians, who for so long did not see their own stories in our national narrative, but who now proudly declare and stand by their contributions and drive the conversations on reconciliation and better lives for their communities.

Yes, we can be confident that the ABC matters. Looking ahead, the challenge is for us to capitalise on these strengths in order to serve the nation into the future.

The first priority is to make sure we stay committed to our point of difference in the world: Australia. To do this, we need to *look and sound like the modern Australia* that I described earlier: a nation with a vastly bigger and more diverse population, one that is more mobile and agile and inclusive, one that faces old and new pressures in managing modern life. As fast as we can, we are driving diversity in all that we do—in our presenters and program-makers, in the perspectives and stories we tell. It's more than the right thing: it will make us more relevant, interesting and exciting to our audiences at home and around the world. Australians are always curious about who we are today as a people and where we are going tomorrow. In facilitating this interest with honesty and optimism, the ABC will help Australians maintain their strong sense of Australian identity for a new era.

The second thing we need to do, and it is related to the first, is to be *more local*. Again, that has been a theme of this book, and it's a mission for the current generation of ABC leaders. By this I mean that we need to tell the stories that matter to Australians where they live, from the new and growing suburbs of families grappling with cost-of-living issues, to growing regional cities like Newcastle, Wollongong and the Gold Coast, to the outback towns and regions whose populations are increasing. We must expand our on-the-ground presence, but also our digital presence and our relevance to every individual. This is what the citizens of Australia need, expect and deserve from us. And it's a democratic imperative. If we are not shining the light of public-interest journalism on the choices facing expanding local communities, or made there, then there is a growing risk of undiscovered malfeasance and mismanagement.

The third agenda item is to become *more personalised*. This does not mean, I assure you, using algorithms to take a simplistic cue from a few of your decisions in order to direct you forever to the same-ish material. Nor does it mean splitting up the ABC experience for individuals into discrete silos and losing that sense of national communion and shared experience that has been so important to the ABC's role in national life. Most Australians experience the ABC through the prism of their unique interests via their preferred channels. But I've tried in these pages to give a sense of the extraordinary range of entertainment, ideas, conversations and culture that we have to offer. We want to help our audiences find more ways to enjoy, learn and be inspired by the ABC's offerings—to get the most out of the ABC that belongs to them. The aim is to broaden and share, not narrow or diminish. And as part of that quest, we will be using some automated processes based on information gathered, with your permission, to help you discover what might be interesting to you. This will always be managed ethically and carefully.

But we also have other ways of personalising— and therefore broadening—the quality of the ABC experience. Our own broadcasters are often experts in their fields and act as 'curators' of interesting, relevant content across everything from health to jazz, from the latest books to the latest theatre, from gardens to astronomy, from local politics to world affairs, and much more. The use of our presenters with their taste-making role sets music radio channels like triple j and ABC Classic well apart from those blunt anonymous algorithmic services. I suspect that one of the big attractions for younger

Australians regarding ABC Classic, for example, is the opportunity to learn more about the art form from friendly and informed presenters.

And we are going to market our offerings more widely and effectively. A friend told me about this amazing ABC podcast they'd come across called *Stuff the British Stole*. They sounded less grateful than mildly irritated: 'It's the most entertaining history-telling I've heard in years. Why wasn't I told about it before?' In fact, *Stuff the British Stole* is one of our most popular podcasts. In each episode, the versatile Marc Fennell picks one artefact, taken from somewhere around the world, and takes listeners on the fascinating story of its journey to a British museum. It's available now on the ABC Listen app, Apple Podcasts, Google Podcasts and more. The ABC offers creativity across so many dimensions, but if we don't tell people about what we make, they can easily miss it in the river of content pouring past them every day.

And our traditional ABC strengths will also continue to serve us well. We have long specialised in live events like Australia Day, ANZAC Day and New Year's Eve that draw mass viewers to the drama of communal and simultaneous Australian experiences. That won't change—in fact, it will become even more of a unique strength. Radio continues to thrive, alongside a boom in podcasts and audiobooks, where the ABC is also very strong.

Ultimately, of course, we have the most powerful asset of all: the ABC brand, which is trusted and recognised as the voice of Australia at its best.

The ideal level of funding for the ABC is always a matter for debate. But it is ultimately about the sort of Australia we want. Do we as a nation believe in the notion of an institution serving all Australians independently, with a broad charter to provide services that the private sector cannot possibly fulfil? I believe we do.

In this, the ABC's ninetieth year, we have an opportunity as a nation to celebrate its significant achievements and contributions. Over this time, the ABC has faced challenges in each and every decade, and overcome them, prospering in the national interest. We also look to the future. As I look ahead, I see the ABC as the most trusted media source in the country, an institution that promotes good citizenship, contributes to our national identity, and fortifies our democracy. The ABC as an indispensable resource for Australians everywhere, telling Australian stories that everyone knows and loves, reaching the highest digital audience of any Australian provider. An organisation that is adaptable, optimistic and brave, transformed inside and out to enable us to keep pace with a fast-changing, ever-evolving and disruptive media landscape. An ABC that will strongly appeal to increasingly bigger, broader and more diverse audiences. An ABC that reflects our nation's rich, evolving and diverse character back to itself, turbocharging our national creative and cultural power. An ABC Australia loves, trusts, values and relies upon more than ever. An ABC that will thrive for generations to come.

ACKNOWLEDGEMENTS

Dedicated to the ABC's audiences, across Australia, everywhere.

This book is the result of conversations with my ABC colleagues, speeches I have given, interviews, and regular appearances before the Australian Senate. It was made possible because of the engagement and input of many ABC people, and particularly my public affairs team. My sincere thanks also go to Louise Adler, who invited me to be part of this important Monash University Publishing series, and to Paul Smitz for his editorial care.

NOTES

1   Analysis by The Australian Newsroom Mapping Project, 2021, https://anmp.piji.com.au (viewed November 2021).

2   Margaret Lyons, 'The Best TV Episodes of 2020', *The New York Times*, 17 December 2020, https://www.nytimes.com/2020/12/17/arts/television/best-tv-episodes.html (viewed November 2021).

3   *Guardian*, 2 June 2020.

4   Ita Buttrose, 'Heywire Gala Dinner Address', ABC, 13 February 2020, https://about.abc.net.au/speeches/heywire-gala-dinner-address (viewed November 2021).

5   Bianca De Marchi, 'COVID Has Made One Thing Very Clear: We Do Not Know Enough about Australians Overseas', *The Conversation*, 6 May 2021, https://theconversation.com/covid-has-made-one-thing-very-clear-we-do-not-know-enough-about-australians-overseas-159995 (viewed November 2021).

6   Australian Bureau of Statistics, 'Regional Internal Migration Estimates, Provisional', 3 August 2021, https://www.abs.gov.au/statistics/people/population/regional-internal-migration-estimates-provisional/latest-release (viewed November 2021).

7   Australia Wide First Aid, 'Life Expectancy in Australia', 22 July 2021, https://www.australiawidefirstaid.com.au/resources/life-expectancy-australia (viewed November 2021).

8   See the Australian Parliamentary Education Office explainer at https://peo.gov.au/understand-our-parliament/how-parliament-works/system-of-government/democracy (viewed November 2021).

9   For a survey of the relevant research, see Ken Newton, 'Public Service and Commercial Broadcasting Impacts on Politics and Society', *The Political Quarterly*, vol. 87, no. 1, January–March 2016, pp. 31–8.

10   Peter Doherty, *The Knowledge Wars*, Melbourne University Publishing, 2015, p. 140.

11   Peter Doherty, Twitter, 23 August 2021.

12   Alice Calaprice (ed.), *The Ultimate Quotable Einstein*, Princeton University Press, 1932, p. 102.

13   Robert Skidelsky, *John Maynard Keynes*, vol. 3, *Fighting for Freedom, 1937–1946*, Viking Adult, New York, 2001, p. 294.

14   Matthijs Baas, Bernard A Nijstad and Carsten KW De Dreu, 'Editorial: "The Cognitive, Emotional and Neural Correlates of Creativity"', *Frontiers in Human Neuroscience*, 19 May 2015, https://doi.org/10.3389/fnhum.2015.00275 (viewed November 2021).

15   Radwa Khalil, Ben Godde and Ahmed A Karim, 'The Link between Creativity, Cognition, and Creative Drives and Underlying Neural Mechanisms', *Frontiers in Neural Circuits*, 22 March 2019, https://doi.org/10.3389/fncir.2019.00018 (viewed November 2021).

16   Gayle Austin, 'The Origins of Double J: Gayle Austin', Radioinfo, 1 May 2014, https://radioinfo.com.au/news/origins-double-j-gayle-austin (viewed November 2021).

IN THE NATIONAL INTEREST

Other books on the issues that matter:

Bill Bowtell *Unmasked: The Politics of Pandemics*

Michael Bradley *System Failure: The Silencing of Rape Survivors*

Samantha Crompvoets *Blood Lust, Trust & Blame*

Satyajit Das *Fortune's Fool: Australia's Choices*

Richard Denniss *Big: The Role of the State in the Modern Economy*

Rachel Doyle *Power & Consent*

Jo Dyer *Burning Down the House: Reconstructing Modern Politics*

Wayne Errington & Peter van Onselen
Who Dares Loses: Pariah Policies

Gareth Evans *Good International Citizenship:
The Case for Decency*

Carrillo Gantner *Dismal Diplomacy, Disposable Sovereignty:
Our Problem with China & America*

Kate Fitz-Gibbon *Our National Shame: Violence against Women*

Paul Fletcher *Governing in the Internet Age*

Jill Hennessy *Respect*

John Lyons *Dateline Jerusalem: Journalism's Toughest Assignment*

Richard Marles *Tides that Bind: Australia in the Pacific*

Fiona McLeod *Easy Lies & Influence*

Louise Newman *Rape Culture*

Martin Parkinson *A Decade of Drift*

Abul Rizvi *Population Shock*

Kevin Rudd *The Case for Courage*

Don Russell *Leadership*

Scott Ryan *Challenging Politics*

Kate Thwaites & Jenny Macklin *Enough Is Enough*

Simon Wilkie *The Digital Revolution: A Survival Guide*